Beach

MW01170660

Celebrating the Beach with Rhymes, Songs, Projects, Games, and Snacks

Written and Compiled by ELIZABETH MCKINNON
Illustrated by MARION HOPPING EKBERG

Totline® Publications
A Division of Frank Schaffer Publications, Inc.
Torrance, California

Totline Publications would like to thank the following people for their contributions to this book: Sr. Mary Bezold, Corbin, KY; John M. Bittinger, Everett, WA; Cherise F. Crawford-Cotter, Garden Grove, CA; Cindy Dingwall, Palatine, IL; Debra Lindahl, Libertyville, IL; Susan Peters, Upland, CA; Evelyn Petersen, Traverse City, MI; Dawn Picolelli, Wilmington, DE; Lois E. Putnam, Pilot Mt., NC; Beverly Qualheim, Manitowoc, WI; Betty Silkunas, New Wales, PA; Jeannette Sweet, Newport Beach, CA; Diane Thom, Maple Valley, WA; Barbara Wider, Old Field, NY; Robyn Wilmoth, Warren, OH; Rebecca D. Wilson, Naples, FL; Angela Wolfe-Batten, Dayton, OH.

Managing Editor: Mina McMullin

Contributing Editors: Durby Peterson, Jean Warren

Copyeditor: Kathy Zaun

Editorial Assistant: Mary Newmaster

Graphic Designer (Interior): Jill Kaufman

Graphic Designer (Cover): Brenda Mann Harrison

Production Manager: Janie Schmidt

ISBN: 1-57029-274-4

Printed in the United States of America
Published by Totline® Publications
23740 Hawthorne Blvd.
Torrance, CA 90505

Contents

Introduction

Summertime is the perfect time for you and your child to enjoy beach play—whether at the seashore, at a freshwater park with lots of sand, or in your own backyard.

Beach Days is filled with activities that invite your child to have fun with sand, water, seashells, and more.

A glance through the book shows you a creative mix of ideas—beach songs and rhymes to learn with your child, fun art and science projects for your child to do, games your child can play with you and with friends, and snacks inspired by the beach to prepare and enjoy together.

While some of the activities can be done at a sandy beach, all of them are designed for doing at home. All you will need are tubs of sand and water—or a sandbox and a wading pool—plus some seashells and ordinary materials that are readily available. (For bags of clean sand, check plant nurseries. For shells, look in craft stores or import shops.)

Playing with sand and water is always fun for young children, and your child is sure to want to enjoy some free play. You can encourage this by providing a few of the common household items listed on the following page for your child to use as sand and water toys.

Sand Toys

- variety of plastic containers
- measuring cups and spoons
- funnels
- scoops
- sieve
- spray bottle of water
- gelatin molds
- cookie cutters
- muffin tin
- small pans

Water Toys

- variety of plastic containers
- measuring cups and spoons
- funnels
- small pitcher
- turkey baster
- squeeze bottles
- sponges
- plastic straws
- eggbeater
- whisk

Rhymes & Songs

A Day at the Beach

Whoosh goes the wind.
(Sway arms back and forth.)

Sniff-sniff goes my nose.
(Sniff.)

Crash go the waves.
(Clap.)

Splish-splash go my toes.
(Kick feet.)

I'll hunt for seashells.
(Pretend to gather shells.)

You sift the sand.
(Pretend to sift sand.)

Let's build a castle

As high as we can!
(Place one fist on top of the other, going higher and higher.)

For lunch, we'll have crackers,

Some juice, and a peach.
(Pretend to eat.)

Oh my, what fun

Is this day at the beach!
(Clap hands.)

Adapted Traditional

Beach Song

Sung to: "The Wheels on the Bus"

The sun at the beach is shining bright,
Shining bright, shining bright.
The sun at the beach is shining bright
All through the day.

The waves of the sea come rolling in,
Rolling in, rolling in.
The waves of the sea come rolling in
All through the day.

The seagulls up above come diving down,
Diving down, diving down.
The seagulls up above come diving down
All through the day.

The crabs near the rocks go pinch, pinch, pinch;
Pinch, pinch, pinch; pinch, pinch, pinch.
The crabs near the rocks go pinch, pinch, pinch
All through the day.

The sand underfoot goes crunch, crunch, crunch;
Crunch, crunch, crunch; crunch, crunch, crunch.
The sand underfoot goes crunch, crunch, crunch
All through the day.

The kids at the seashore splash and play,
Splash and play, splash and play.
The kids at the seashore splash and play
All through the day.

Encourage your child to help you make up additional verses.

Cherise F. Crawford-Cotter

Our Sandcastle

Dad and I went down to the beach

To build a castle this high.
   (Place hand at waist level.)

It started out small without many rooms,

But soon, it was touching the sky.
   (Raise hand as high as possible.)

We stayed at the beach in the warm sunshine,

Watching the seagulls all day.
   (Cup hand above eye and look around.)

Then the waves splashed so high up onto the shore

That our castle was all washed away!
   (Swoosh away pretend castle.)

Beverly Qualheim

Make a Sand Cake

Sung to: "Frère Jacques"

Make a sand cake, make a castle

In the sand, in the sand.

Digging and sifting,

Sifting and pouring

Just feels grand, just feels grand.

Betty Silkunas

Sand and Sun

Sung to: "Row, Row, Row Your Boat"

Beach, beach, sand, and sun,
Playing by the sea.
Summertime is just for fun,
A special time for me!

Digging in the sand,
Happy as can be.
Summertime is just for fun,
A special time for me!

Rebecca D. Wilson

Beach Play

Seashells, white sand, ocean blue,
Sunshine, cool breeze, seagulls, too.
Hear the children laugh and shout
As they play and run about.

Angela Wolfe-Batten

I Love Sand

Sung to: "Three Blind Mice"

Sand, sand, sand,
Sand, sand, sand.
I love sand,
I love sand.
It's fun to squish it
Between my toes,
Or build a mountain
As high as my nose,
Or dig a tunnel
That grows and grows,
'Cause I love sand!

Susan Hodges

My Sifter

Have you ever shaken a sifter
A shakity-shake-shake-shake?
Have you ever shaken a sifter
When you're making a big sand cake?

Oh, I like to shake my sifter
A shakity-shake-shake-shake.
Yes, I like to shake my sifter
When I'm making a big sand cake!

Lois E. Putnam

Scoop and Count

Sung to: "Row, Row, Row Your Boat"

Scoop, scoop, scoop the sand,

Scoop it one, two, three.

Scooping, scooping,

Scooping, scooping—

Scoop and count with me.

Count with your child as she scoops sand into a pail.

Elizabeth McKinnon

Digging in the Sand

I dig holes in the sand with my fingers,
   (Wiggle fingers.)

I dig holes in the sand with my toes.
   (Wiggle toes.)

Then I pour some water in the holes—
   (Pretend to pour water.)

I wonder where it goes?
   (Hold hands out to sides, palms up.)

Elizabeth McKinnon

Pretty Seashell

Sung to: "Frère Jacques"

Pretty seashell, pretty seashell

On the sand, on the sand.

Pick it up and hold it,

Pick it up and hold it

In your hand, in your hand.

Sing while gathering seashells with your child.

Elizabeth McKinnon

Seashells

See the little seashells,

Count them one by one.

Line them up upon the sand—

It really is quite fun!

Give your child some seashells and
encourage him to act out the rhyme.

Adapted Traditional

Saw a Crab

Sung to: "Clementine"

I went walking,

I went walking,

Saw a crab

Right on the beach.

Saw a crab,

Saw a crab

Walking this way

With its feet.
   (Walk sideways on hands and feet.)

Cindy Dingwall

I Am a Sea Star

I am a sea star, not a fish.
I'll tell you the difference, if you wish.
Fish have fins and swim in schools,
While I have feet and wade in tide pools.

Yes, indeed, sea star's my name.
Ask me again, and I'll tell you the same.
Fish can swim and splash all day,
But stuck to a rock I'd rather stay.

Explain to your child that sea stars used
to be called *starfish*, but now they are
known by their more accurate name.

John M. Bittinger

The Waves Are Moving

Sung to: "When Johnny Comes Marching Home"

The waves are moving across the sea,

Hurrah, hurrah.

The waves are moving across the sea,

Hurrah, hurrah.

The waves are moving constantly,

They move so fast across the sea.

Oh, the waves are moving fast

Across the sea.

Gayle Bittinger

Water Everywhere

Water, water everywhere,

On my face and on my hair—

On my fingers, on my toes,

Water, water, on my nose!

Jean Warren

Fishy in the Sea

Sung to: "Twinkle, Twinkle, Little Star"

I'm a fishy in the sea

Swimming, oh, so happily.

I'm so fast, and I'm so cute.

I can swim without a suit.

I'm a fishy in the sea

Swimming, oh, so happily.

Robyn Wilmoth

Like a Fish

I hold my fingers like a fish
(Place one hand on top of the other.)

And wave them as I go.
(Wave joined hands.)

See them swimming with a swish
(Swim and flip joined hands in air.)

So swiftly to and fro.
(Swim joined hands back and forth.)

Adapted Traditional

The Jellyfish

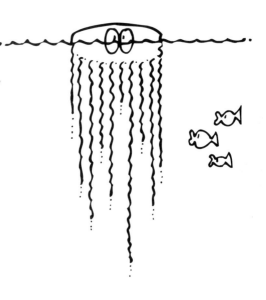

Sung to: "My Bonnie Lies Over the Ocean"

The jellyfish lives in the ocean.

The jellyfish lives in the sea.

The jellyfish lives in the ocean.

Oh, jellyfish, please swim by me.

Swim, swim, swim, swim,

Oh, jellyfish, please swim by me, by me.

Swim, swim, swim, swim,

Oh, jellyfish, please swim by me.

Susan Peters

Sailing

Sung to: "When Johnny Comes Marching Home"

Owen is sailing in a boat

Today, hurray!

Owen is sailing in a boat

Today, hurray!

He's sailing out on the deep blue sea.

Maybe he'll catch a fish for me.

Oh, we'll all watch Owen

Sailing on the sea.

Substitute your child's name for Owen.

Barbara Wider

Just for Fun

Backyard Beach Play

You Will Need

- plastic tubs
- sand
- water
- shells
- beach-play props
- bathing suit
- sunscreen

1. Make a "backyard beach" by setting out plastic tubs of sand and water and adding a few shells.

2. Collect beach-play props, such as a beach towel, a beach umbrella, a sand pail and shovel, a beach ball, sunglasses, a beach hat, swim fins, and a portable radio.

3. Help your child put on a bathing suit and sunscreen.

4. Invite him to use the beach-play props for some pretend beach play.

   Another Idea: For lists of common household items your child can use as sand and water toys, see the introduction.

Sand Tower Toy

You Will Need

sand

water

plastic stacking cups or set of cans that fit one inside the other

1. Invite your child to mix sand and water to make wet sand.

2. Give her a set of plastic stacking cups—the kind sold in toy stores for young children. Or, use a set of empty cans that fit one inside the other.

3. Help her fill each cup to the top with wet sand and pack it down hard.

4. Encourage her to experiment with tower building by unmolding the largest cup first, the next-largest cup second, and so forth, down to the smallest cup. How many cups of sand can she stack? What happens if she starts with the smallest cup of sand? With dry sand?

Another Idea: Provide your child with other sand toys, such as those listed in the introduction. Encourage her to use the toys with both dry and wet sand.

Plastic Bottle Water Toy

You Will Need

20-ounce plastic soft-drink bottle
scissors
nail
water

1. Using scissors, cut the plastic soft-drink bottle in half crosswise and trim any rough edges.

2. Give your child the top part of the bottle to use as a funnel for water play.

3. Turn the bottom part of the bottle upside down. Poke holes in it with a nail to make a "sprinkler."

4. Invite your child to fill the bottom part of the bottle with water and watch it pour out of the holes.

   Another Idea: Provide your child with other water toys, using the list in the introduction for ideas.

Sand Dough

You Will Need

large bowl
measuring cup
flour
salt
water
vegetable oil or liquid dishwashing detergent
sand

1. In a large bowl, combine 2 cups flour, 1 cup salt, 1 cup water, and a few drops vegetable oil or liquid dishwashing detergent.

2. Let your child help knead the mixture to a doughlike consistency.

3. Add ½ to ¾ cup sand to create the desired texture.

4. Invite your child to play with the textured dough, rolling it, poking it, pounding it, and creating with it. Encourage her to describe how the dough feels in her hands.

Colored Sand Painting

You Will Need

sand
small containers
food coloring
white posterboard square
old baking pan
squeeze bottle of glue

1. Pour sand into several small containers, such as plastic margarine tubs.

2. Add drops of different-colored food coloring to the sand in each container and mix well. Allow the sand to dry overnight.

3. Place a white posterboard square in an old baking pan and invite your child to squeeze on glue designs.

4. Help him sprinkle one color of sand over the glue and tap off the excess back into the pan. Pour the excess sand back into its container (save for other projects, if you wish).

5. Invite your child to squeeze more glue designs onto his posterboard square and sprinkle on a different color of sand.

6. Have him continue in the same manner until his sand painting is completed. Allow it to dry thoroughly before displaying his creation.

   Another Idea: Instead of squeezing on glue, let your child use cotton swabs to paint on glue designs.

Sand Casting

You Will Need

    small beach or nature items
    ruler
    sand
    disposable aluminum pie pan
    plaster of Paris
    water

1. Let your child collect small beach items or other nature items, such as shells, shell pieces, pebbles, twigs, and dried moss.

2. Have her spread about 1 inch of sand in the bottom of a disposable aluminum pie pan and arrange her nature items on top of the sand.

3. Mix plaster of Paris with water, following the package directions, and carefully pour the mixture over the sand and nature items. Allow the plaster to dry overnight.

4. When the plaster is completely dry, help your child turn the pan upside down, remove the hardened plaster, and brush off the sand to reveal a casting of her nature items.

Beach Scene

You Will Need

blue construction paper
glue
shallow container
paintbrush
sand
small shells
scissors
yellow construction paper

1. Give your child a piece of blue construction paper and some glue poured into a shallow container.

2. Invite him to make a beach by brushing the glue over the bottom part of his paper and sprinkling on sand.

3. Have him dip small shells into the glue and add them to his beach.

4. To complete his Beach Scene, give him a sun shape cut from yellow construction paper to glue at the top of his paper.

Beach Mobile

You Will Need

construction paper   sand

scissors   heavy thread or string

ruler   coat hanger

crayons or markers   tape (optional)

glue

1. From construction paper, cut out several 3- to 4-inch beach shapes, such as a fish, a crab, a sea star, and some shells.

2. Let your child use crayons or markers to decorate both sides of the shapes. Also have her glue on a little sand.

3. Make a mobile frame by tying various lengths of heavy thread or string to the bottom of a coat hanger.

4. Tape or tie your child's beach shapes to the ends of the thread or string.

5. Hang her Beach Mobile in a place where the shapes can freely twirl in the air.

Shell Collage

You Will Need

shells
sturdy paper plate or square of cardboard
glue
shallow container
sand (optional)

1. Help your child collect shells at the beach. Or, purchase shells from a craft store or an import shop.

2. Give him a sturdy paper plate or a square of cardboard.

3. Pour glue into a shallow container.

4. Invite your child to dip the shells into the glue and arrange them on the paper plate or cardboard square to make a Shell Collage.

5. While the glue is still wet, encourage him to add a little sand to his collage, if he wishes. Allow the collage to dry thoroughly before displaying it.

Dot-Print Sea Star

You Will Need

light- and dark-colored construction paper
pen
ruler
colored ink pad
brand-new pencil with eraser on end
child-safe scissors
glue

1. On a piece of light-colored construction paper, draw a large sea star shape, about 8 inches across, as shown in the illustration.

2. Give your child a colored ink pad and a brand-new pencil with an eraser on the end.

3. Have her press the eraser onto the ink pad and use it like a rubber stamp to make dot prints all over her sea star shape, overlapping the prints and filling in the shape completely.

4. When she has finished, help her cut out her decorated shape and lightly attach it with glue to a piece of dark-colored construction paper for displaying on a wall or a door.

Yarn Fish

You Will Need

scissors
bright colors of yarn
ruler
bright blue construction paper
glue
small plastic moving eyes

1. Cut various bright colors of yarn into pieces, about 7 to 11 inches long.

2. Give your child a piece of bright blue construction paper.

3. Show him how to form the yarn pieces into simple fish shapes, as shown in the illustration, and glue them onto his paper.

4. To complete his Yarn Fish, have him glue a small plastic moving eye inside each one.

Paper Plate Fish

You Will Need

thin white paper plate
pen
child-safe scissors
glue
markers or paint and paintbrush

1. Find a thin white paper plate and draw a triangular shape at one edge.

2. Help your child cut out the shape, which leaves an opening to represent the fish's mouth.

3. Show her how to glue the triangular piece to the edge opposite the mouth to create the fish's tail, as shown in the illustration.

4. Let her complete her Paper Plate Fish by coloring it with markers or paint and drawing on an eye.

   Another Idea: Invite your child to decorate her fish by tearing colored tissue paper into small pieces and gluing them on for "scales."

Swimming Jellyfish

You Will Need

child-safe scissors
white posterboard
white tissue paper
glue
string

1. For a jellyfish body, cut a large half circle out of white posterboard.

2. Using child-safe scissors, help your child cut white tissue paper into long, thin strips.

3. Have him glue the ends of the strips to the back of the jellyfish body, along the straight edge, for "tentacles."

4. Hang his completed jellyfish from the ceiling or on a string stretched across a window. Watch as it "swims" in the room's air currents.

Underwater Picture

You Will Need

white construction paper
crayons
blue tempera paint
shallow container
water
paintbrush or sponge piece

1. Give your child a piece of white construction paper and some bright-colored crayons.

2. Invite her to draw an underwater scene, including such things as fish, shells, sand, and seaweed. Encourage her to press down hard while she is coloring.

3. Pour blue tempera paint into a shallow container and dilute it with a small amount of water.

4. Have your child use a paintbrush or a sponge piece to cover her paper with the blue paint, making her scene appear to be floating underwater.

5. When the paint has dried, display her Underwater Picture on a wall or a door.

Another Idea: For a more dramatic effect, let your child draw with fluorescent crayons.

Making Sand

You Will Need

plastic jar with lid
water
rocks
shells

1. Explain to your child that sand is made from rocks and shells that have been ground down by water into tiny pieces. Invite him to try making a few grains of sand with this experiment.

2. Fill a plastic jar partway full with water and have him add several small rocks and shells. Tightly screw on the jar lid.

3. Encourage your child to shake the jar as hard as he can to make "waves."

4. Have him continue until the shells start breaking into small pieces and he can see a few small grains of sand at the bottom of the jar.

Wave Bottle

You Will Need

    clear-plastic soft-drink bottle with cap
    water
    blue food coloring
    mineral oil
    waterproof glue

1. Fill the clear-plastic soft-drink bottle about two-thirds full with water. Use drops of food coloring to tint the water blue.

2. Add mineral oil to the bottle to fill it to the top, leaving no room for air bubbles to form.

3. Tightly screw the cap on the bottle and secure it with waterproof glue.

4. Invite your child to hold the bottle sideways and gently rock it back and forth to make "waves."

Buried Treasure

You Will Need

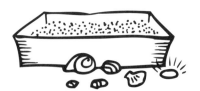

two or more players
treasure
small shells
sandbox or tub of sand

1. Select a "treasure," such as a shiny penny or a small rock that you have painted gold, plus eight to ten small shells. Show the items to the players.

2. Have them close their eyes while you bury the treasure and the shells in a sandbox or a plastic tub of sand.

3. When the players open their eyes, invite them to take turns digging with their hands for the buried items.

4. After all the items have been found, let the player who discovered the treasure bury the items for the next round of the game.

Beach Ball Fun

You Will Need

four or more players
beach ball

1. Invite your child and her friends to stand in a circle. Choose one player to be It.

2. Invite It to stand in the middle of the circle, toss a beach ball into the air, and call out, "Beach ball for (name of a player in the circle)!"

3. Have the player who is named retrieve the ball. Then designate that child as the new It.

4. Continue the game until everyone has had a turn tossing the ball and retrieving it.

Shell Game

You Will Need

one or more players
paper cups
small shell

1. Place two paper cups next to each other, upside down, on a smooth surface.

2. Invite your child to watch as you slide a small shell under one of the cups, then move the cups around several times.

3. Ask him to guess which cup the shell is under. Lift the cup. Was his guess correct? If not, show him where the shell was hidden.

4. Repeat the game several times.

5. When your child is ready for a new challenge, add a third cup to the lineup. As he becomes more skilled, try moving the cups around more times or a little faster each time you play.

Squirt!

You Will Need

one or more players
crayons
paper plate
squirt bottle
water

1. Use crayons to draw a sea star on a paper plate.

2. Place the plate on the ground or hang it on a fence.

3. Fill a squirt bottle, such as a liquid dishwashing detergent bottle, with water.

4. With your child, stand a few feet from the paper plate and take turns squirting water at the sea star target.

5. As your child becomes skilled at hitting the target, have her move back a step or two and continue playing.

Crab Walk

You Will Need

one or more players
small prizes

1. In an open, grassy area, set up a start line and a finish line.

2. Have your child get down on his hands and knees at the start line, pretending to be a little crab.

3. At the count of three, have him start crawling sideways toward the finish line.

4. When he crosses the finish line, give him a small prize, such as a gummy fish, a shell, or a paper sea star shape.

5. Repeat the game as long as interest lasts.

   Another Idea: Encourage older children to try the traditional Crab Walk. Ask them to sit on the ground and lean back on their hands. Have them bend their knees, keeping their feet flat on the ground. Then have them lift their bottoms off the ground and try moving sideways.

Jellyfish, Don't Touch Me!

You Will Need

three or more players
tape
crepe-paper streamers
yarn

1. Make "jellyfish tentacles" by taping crepe-paper streamers to a piece of yarn that is long enough to tie around a child's waist.

2. Designate your child as the Jellyfish and tie on her tentacles. Let the other players be Fish.

3. As the Fish "swim" around in a large open area, have the Jellyfish chase them and try to touch them with her tentacles.

4. Whenever she touches a Fish, have that player stand still.

5. Continue until all the Fish have stopped swimming. Let the last one to be touched be the Jellyfish for the next round of the game.

Sandy Treat

vanilla pudding
graham cracker

1. Give your child a small cup of vanilla pudding.

2. Help him put a graham cracker inside a small resealable plastic bag and zip it closed.

3. Have him hold the bag in his hands and crush the graham cracker inside it.

4. Invite him to open the bag and sprinkle his cracker crumbs on top of the pudding for "sand."

   Another Idea: Instead of using a graham cracker, let your child make "sand" by crushing one or two vanilla cookies.

Ocean Waves

blue gelatin
blue food coloring
whipped topping
gummy fish

1. Prepare blue gelatin according to the package directions.

2. Pour the gelatin into clear-plastic cups and allow it to set in the refrigerator.

3. Use food coloring to tint whipped topping light blue.

4. Invite your child to help spoon the topping onto the cups of blue gelatin to create "waves" and add gummy fish for decorations.

5. Serve right away (have your child remove the gummy fish to eat separately).

Seashell Salad

3 cups small pasta shells
water
1 can tuna, flaked
1/8 cup chopped pickles
1/8 cup diced celery
1/8 cup green onion
1/8 cup grated carrot
4 Tbs. mayonnaise
1 Tbs. mustard
1/2 cup grated cheese

1. Cook pasta shells according to the package directions. Drain and let cool in cold water.

2. In a large bowl, combine tuna, pickles, celery, green onion, carrot, mayonnaise, and mustard.

3. Drain pasta shells again and stir them into the tuna mixture.

4. Spoon salad into small bowls. Let your child help sprinkle on small amounts of grated cheese before serving.

Another Idea: Substitute French, Ranch, or Thousand Island salad dressing for the mayonnaise and mustard.

Tuna Fishwiches

slices of firm bread
tuna fish
mayonnaise
black olive slices

1. Using a cookie cutter or a sharp knife, cut fish shapes out of slices of firm bread.

2. Let your child help mix tuna fish with a small amount of mayonnaise.

3. Spread the tuna mixture on the bread fish shapes.

4. Invite your child to add a black olive slice to each fish for an eye.

Fish in the Sea

split pea soup
blue food coloring (optional)
fish crackers

1. Heat split pea soup according to the package directions.

2. To make it more "ocean"-colored, add a small amount of blue food coloring to the soup, if you wish.

3. Spoon the soup into small cups. Let your child add several small fish crackers to each cup.

4. Serve right away with extra fish crackers on the side.

Celery Sailboat

celery
peanut butter
stick pretzel
paper sail shape

1. Invite your child to fill a 4-inch-long piece of celery with peanut butter.

2. Let her stand a stick pretzel in the peanut butter for a mast.

3. Cut out a paper sail shape, punch two holes in it, and gently slip it over the mast, as shown in the illustration.

4. Have your child remove the paper sail before eating her Celery Sailboat.

   Another Idea: Let your child decorate her paper sail with crayons or markers before attaching it to the mast.